LIFE
ISN'T ABOUT
finding
Yourself.

LIFE
IS ABOUT
Creating
Yourself.

— George Bernard Shaw

A TRUE ARTIST **is** NOT ONE WHO is INSPIRED, BUT ONE WHO INSPIRES OTHERS.

— Salvador Dali

I BELIEVE

The most **IMPORTANT** single Thing, **BEYOND** Discipline AND **CREATIVITY**, is daring **TO DARE**.

—Maya Angelou

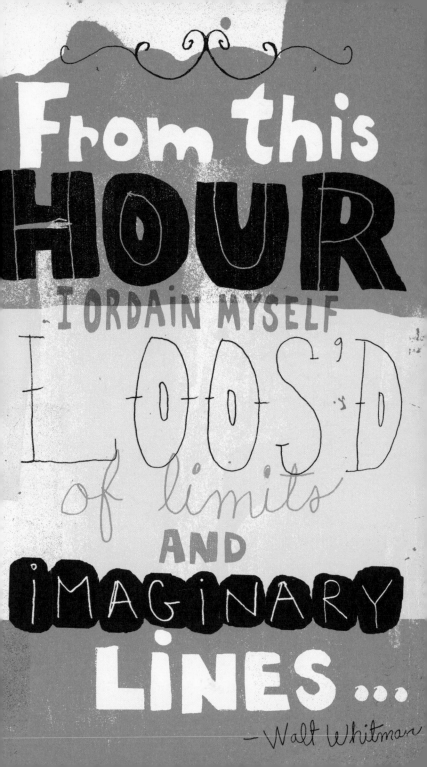

CREATIVITY

is

INTELLIGENCE

HAVING

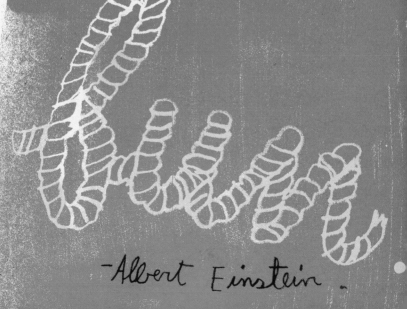

fun

-Albert Einstein.

THE ARTIST
MUST POSSESS *the courageous* SOUL THAT DARES and DEFIES.

— Kate Chopin

I WISH for YOU A
WRESTLING MATCH with your
CREATIVE MUSE that will last a
•LIFETIME.•
I WISH CRAZINESS AND
FOOLishness
AND MADNESS UPON YOU.
⇒May you live with HYSTERIA,
and out of it MAKE FINE STORIES...
WHICH finally MEANS,
MAY YOU BE 2/IN LOVE
every day for THE NEXT 20,000 DAYS.
AND out of that Love,
REMAKE A WORLD.

— Ray Bradbury